5/14

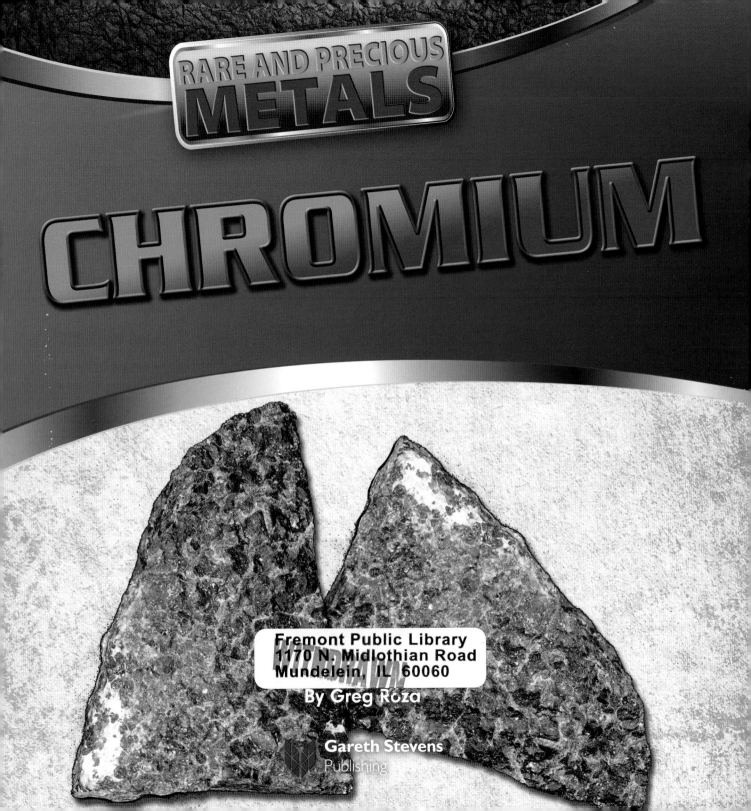

RARE AND PRECIOUS METALS

CHROMIUM

By Greg Roza

Gareth Stevens
Publishing

Please visit our website, www.garethstevens.com. For a free color catalog of all our high-quality books, call toll free 1-800-542-2595 or fax 1-877-542-2596.

Library of Congress Cataloging-in-Publication Data

Roza, Greg.
Chromium / by Greg Roza.
 p. cm. — (Rare and precious metals)
Includes index.
ISBN 978-1-4824-0490-6 (pbk.)
ISBN 978-1-4824-0491-3 (6-pack)
ISBN 978-1-4824-0487-6 (library binding)
1. Chromium — Juvenile literature. 2. Chemical elements — Juvenile literature. I. Roza, Greg. II. Title.
QD181.C7 R69 2014
546.532—dc23

First Edition

Published in 2014 by
Gareth Stevens Publishing
111 East 14th Street, Suite 349
New York, NY 10003

Copyright © 2014 Gareth Stevens Publishing

Designer: Nicholas Domiano
Editor: Therese Shea

Photo credits: Cover, p. 1 BIOPHOTO ASSOCIATES/Photo Researchers/Getty Images; cover,
pp. 1 (background), 17 iStockphoto/Thinkstock.com; inset Graphic: Aleksandr Bryliaev/Shutterstock.com; caption
box: Hemera/Thinkstock.com; p. 5 photo courtesy of Wikimedia Commons/Alchemist-hp; p. 7 Joel Arem/
Photo Researchers/Getty Images; p. 9 photo courtesy of Wikimedia Commons/CC-BY-2.0; p. 11 Tim Roberts
Photography/Shutterstock.com; p. 13 Graeme Williams/Gallo Images/Getty Images; p. 15 hddigital/Shutterstock.
com; p. 19 Anton Balazh/Shutterstock.com; p. 20 Imfoto/Shutterstock.com.

Printed in the United States of America

CPSIA compliance information: Batch #CW14GS: For further information contact Gareth Stevens, New York, New York at 1-800-542-2595.

Contents

Words in the glossary appear in **bold** type the first time they are used in the text.

What Are Metals?

Metals are **elements** found in Earth's **crust**. Most are shiny. Many are malleable, which means they can be shaped. Others are **brittle**. Metals are often very good at carrying, or conducting, electricity.

Iron and aluminum are very common metals. They're found in many places around the globe. Other metals, such as chromium, are less common, harder to find, and have more value. Pure chromium is a hard, grayish metal. Scientists have come up with amazing uses for rare and precious metals like chromium.

METAL MANIA!

Some metals came to Earth in hunks of rock that crashed into the planet many years ago!

When chromium is rubbed with a cloth, or polished, it gets very shiny.

5

Chromite

Earth's crust is made up of many different elements. Some of the ones you probably know about are oxygen and iron. Chromium is far less common. However, there's enough chromium in Earth's crust to last us a long time.

Chromium is rarely found pure in nature. It's mostly found in a **mineral** called chromite (KROH-myt), which is chromium's only important **ore**. Chromite is made up of the elements iron, chromium, oxygen, and often magnesium. Chromite is black, silvery black, or brownish-black.

METAL MANIA!

Each human being has a tiny bit of chromium in their body. Scientists think chromium may help the body break down natural sugars. However, too much chromium in the body can be deadly.

The mineral chromite, shown in a large chunk here, may form as bands or spots in rocks.

7

Deposits

Native chromium, or the pure metal found in nature, is rare. Today, the largest native **deposits** are found in a diamond mine in Russia.

The largest chromite deposits are in South Africa. South Africa mines millions of tons of the ore each year. Kazakhstan and India are major sources of chromite, too. However, neither of them mines even half of what South Africa does! Other countries with notable chromite deposits include Turkey, Oman, Russia, Finland, and China.

METAL MANIA!

Because chromite holds up under high temperatures, it's commonly used to line the ovens found in steel foundries. A foundry is a factory that melts metal and shapes it into usable forms.

Although there are chromite mines in Oregon and Montana (shown here), the United States is better known for making products from chromium.

9

Mining

Over millions of years, liquid chromium from Earth's center oozed up and cooled in Earth's crust. This formed chromite deposits. Today, mining companies dig into the crust and remove the ore.

Some chromite is far below Earth's surface. Workers need to dig tunnels to reach it. Chromite close to the surface is collected through open-pit mining. A wide area of earth is scooped out, and the ore is separated from it. Then, another layer is scooped out. In time, this process creates a deep, wide pit.

METAL MANIA!

In 2011, the United States produced 162,000 tons (147,000 mt) of chromium from recycling stainless steel.

Large open-pit mines can be more than a mile (1.6 km) wide!

11

Refining and Mixing

Since native chromium is so rare, chromite is the most available source. Before people can use chromium, it must be separated from chromite. Separating an element from an ore is a process called refining.

Chromium is most useful when mixed with iron. This mixture is an **alloy** called ferrochromium. To produce ferrochromium, chromite is placed in an oven that can reach very high temperatures. The chromite melts, and the iron and chromium **blend** together. When this mixture cools, solid ferrochromium alloy forms.

METAL MANIA!

It's not easy to refine chromium. First, chromite is crushed, combined with other elements, mixed with water, and then dried. Next, it's mixed with aluminum and set on fire! This produces pure chromium.

The chromium and iron alloy is called ferrochromium because the Latin word for iron is *ferrum*.

13

Discovery and Early Uses

In the 1770s, a mineral called "Siberian red lead" was used to color paints. In 1797, French scientist Nicolas-Louis Vauquelin discovered that the colorful mineral contained a new metal. He soon became the first person to separate pure chromium from an ore.

For many years, chromium was mainly used to produce red, yellow, orange, and green **pigments** for the manufacturing of paints and fabrics. A **chemical** called potassium dichromate has long been used to treat, or tan, leather.

METAL MANIA!

Minerals that contain chromium can be very colorful. Because of that, Vauquelin used the Greek word for color—*chroma*—to name the newly discovered element.

Today, we call Siberian red lead "crocoite" (KROH-koh-ite).

15

Supermetal!

Today, chromium is most often used to make other metals better. Chrome is a thin layer of chromium over another metal. Chrome can be polished to look shiny, but it's **durable**, too! It **protects** the metal underneath from rust and other harm.

Chromium is used to make several important alloys. They don't melt until heated to very high temperatures, don't rust easily, and are very hard. These features make them valuable to manufacturers. Most chromium is used to make ferrochromium, and most ferrochromium is used to make stainless steel.

METAL MANIA!

Nichrome is an alloy of iron, chromium, and nickel. It can hold up in very high temperatures, and it's used to make ovens.

Chrome gives a shiny look to cars and keeps them from rusting quickly in bad weather conditions.

17

Stainless Steel

Iron has one major weakness: rust. This happens when oxygen and water in the air join with iron. Stainless steel is an alloy of iron, chromium, carbon, and sometimes other elements. When oxygen joins with the chromium in stainless steel, a protective outer layer results. This keeps rust from forming. It also prevents scratches and other harm.

Jewelry made from stainless steel is inexpensive and durable. Other products made from stainless steel include kitchenware, building supplies, cars, bikes, surgical tools, and much more!

METAL MANIA!

The protective layer that chromium and oxygen form is called chromium oxide.

Stainless steel may be strong, but it can rust, too. It just takes much longer to rust than iron and other metals.

Colorful Chromium

Chromium isn't just used to make alloys. Chemicals containing chromium are still added to pigments. Some chromium chemicals start reactions between other chemicals. These are called catalysts.

Vauquelin discovered that chromium gives some of Earth's most precious gems their beautiful color. Chromium makes the mineral beryl turn a brilliant green—this is where emeralds come from. When chromium is added to the colorless mineral corundum, red rubies are made. Without chromium, Earth wouldn't be able to make these rare and precious gems.

Chromium in Our World

Chromium

- **alloys**
  - stainless steel
  - ferrochromium
  - nichrome
- **chemicals**
  - pigments
  - leather tanning
  - catalysts
- **jewelry**
  - emeralds and rubies
  - stainless steel rings, necklaces, etc.
- **foundry**
  - oven bricks
- **chrome**

21

Glossary

alloy: matter made of two or more metals, or a metal and a nonmetal, melted together

blend: to mix two or more things together so they can't be easily separated

brittle: likely to break or crack

chemical: matter that can be mixed with other matter to cause changes

crust: Earth's outer shell

deposit: an amount of a mineral in the ground that built up over a period of time

durable: able to withstand wear and damage

element: matter, such as chromium, that is pure and has no other type of matter in it

mineral: matter in the ground that forms rocks

ore: matter in the ground from which a valuable metal can be removed

pigment: matter added to something to give it color

protect: to keep safe

For More Information

Books

Hyde, Natalie. *Life in a Mining Community*. New York, NY: Crabtree Publishing, 2010.

Montgomerie, Adrienne. *Metals*. St. Catharines, Ontario: Crabtree Publishing Company, 2013.

Morris, Neil. *Metals*. Mankato, MN: Amicus, 2011.

Websites

Metals for Kids
www.sciencekids.co.nz/metals.html
Find out a lot more about metals. This metals website features photos, videos, quizzes, and experiments.

Periodic Table
www.ducksters.com/science/periodic_table.php
Learn more about chromium and all the other elements of the periodic table.

Index